MW01008119

BALLAD OF THE BONES

Ballad

of the

Bones

and Other Poems

BYRON HERBERT REECE

Introduction by JESSE STUART

 Cherokee Publishing Company
Atlanta, Georgia
1985

Library of Congress Cataloging-in-Publication Data

Reece, Byron Herbert, 1917-1958.
    Ballad of the bones and other poems.

    Reprint. Originally published: New York: E. P. Dutton, 1945.
    I. Title.
PS3535.E245B3   1985   811'.54   85-21338
ISBN 0-87797-100-5 (alk. paper)

This book is printed on acid-free paper which conforms to the American National Standard Z39.48-1984 *Permanence of Paper for Printed Library Materials.* Paper that conforms to this standard's requirements for pH, alkaline reserve and freedom from groundwood is anticipated to last several hundred years without significant deterioration under normal library use and storage conditions. ∞

Manufactured in the United States of America

ISBN: 0-87797-100-5

Published by arrangement with
E. P. Dutton, a division of New American Library

Cherokee Publishing Company
P O Box 1730, Marietta, Ga 30061

For JUAN *and* EMMA

CONTENTS

I

II

CONTENTS

III

IV

ACKNOWLEDGMENT

THANKS are due the editors of the following publications for permission to reprint certain of these poems: *American Poet; Destinies; Kaleidograph; New Mexico Quarterly Review; Poetry Chap-Book; Prairie Schooner; Poetry World; Poet Laureate; Span; New York Herald Tribune* ("A Week of Verse"); *The Washington Post* and *Three Lyric Poets.*

INTRODUCTION

ONE winter evening when I was reading the *Prairie Schooner*, I came across a ballad, "Lest the Lonesome Bird." And, being a native of a section of America where the ballad is still a popular form of expression, even among people who cannot read and write their names, I knew there was something of the mood, something of the very life, blood and thought of these old Americans in this ballad.

Here was someone by the name of Byron Herbert Reece speaking for a people of old American tradition who, owing to the lack of schools and natural barriers, have not taken to our modern civilization as rapidly as the peoples in other sections of our country. I read this ballad several times. There was something in the mood and core of it that stuck in my brain and heart like a good piece of music I can hear over and over again. And I had to write to this author to find out if he had written more ballads; if he had, would he be kind enough to send them to me.

The following week I got this sheaf of poems and his letter that accompanied them to Riverton, Kentucky. In the combined store and post office, crowded as it was with customers, I sat on a potato box and read the entire sheaf and wished his output were more.

"Ballad of the Bones," "Fox Hunters of Hell," "Lest the Lonesome Bird," "Ballad of Coulson's Wood," "May Margaret," "Ballad of the Weaver," "Ballad of the Bride," and "Ballad of the Rider" I read many times. And I thought the "Ballad of the Rider" one of the best ballads by an American poet I had ever read. And then I read his brief lyric poems and thought them very good but not up to the high standard of his ballads.

Not any of the younger poets in America had given me poetry I had enjoyed as much as that of Byron Herbert Reece. For here was a poet who had something to say and he had said it well in one of the very oldest forms of writing. He hadn't written just so many meaningless lines; but he had written lyrical ballads with beauty and power. He had written poetry akin to the sixteenth and seventeenth century English and the early Irish poets.

What my judgment for poetry is worth, I don't know. But I know these poems held me while the customers pushed around me, stepping on my toes, trying to get waited on while I sat there obstructing their passageway. Here, I thought, is a poet.

And this is just his beginning.

JESSE STUART

BALLAD OF THE BONES

BALLAD OF THE BONES

Ezekiel, 37: 1–10

I

As I sat a-drowse
At my very meek board,
Why, who should arouse
Me from sleep but the Lord.

He entered my garret
As a wind from the north,
And in the spirit
Carried me forth

Over tower and town
Of cobbles and stones,
And He set me down
In a valley of bones.

The bones were as dry
As grass in a drought,
And He said: "Pass by
Them round about."

And I passed by
And the white bones lay
As brittle and dry
As shards of clay.

And I passed by
And the bones were strewed
Brittle and dry,
And a multitude.

15

Shin bones here
And thigh bones there,
And arm bones, sere,
And skull bones, bare!

II

O I stood alone
At this very large grave
Where bone from his bone
Was fugitive
— And the Lord: "Ezekiel,
Can these bones live?"

My mind's *ha, ha!*
Had a scornful ring,
But I clamped my jaw
On such a thing!

Shall a bone that has lain
Till the flesh is gone
Be quickened again
To a living bone?

Bones bent like a bow
And fugitive?
I thought, *no, no,*
They cannot live!

But I bowed my head
And my thoughts in accord,
And trembled and said:
"Thou knowest, Lord!"

I shook, as the wind
Of the Lord went blowing,
As boneless and blind
As water flowing;

But His voice said
When the blow was by:
"Lift up thy head
And prophesy.

"Thou raiser of stones
To the power of death,
Say unto these bones,
'Ye shall draw your breath!' "
I said to the bones:
"Ye shall draw your breath!"

"Thou shaker of thrones
By the power I give,
Speak unto these bones
That they may live!"
I said to the bones:
"Thy God says, live!"

"Soothsayer of men,
Say on, say on,
Call flesh and skin
To cover the bone!"
I said: "Flesh, skin,
Come, cover the bone!"

"Ezekiel,
My Truth, My Rod,

These bones shall live
To call me God!"

Something stirred
And I lost my voice;
I heard, I heard
A little noise!

I heard small moans
As the wind would make,
And I looked — and the bones
Began to shake!

As dry as faggots
And dull and dun,
And thick as maggots
In carrion,

With the sound of wind
In icy weather
The bones came rattling
All together!

From among the stones
As dark as soot,
The little bones
To make a foot,

With nought to teach
Them to their place,
Came each to each
In an empty space!

And from the stones,
As clean as a peg,
The larger bones
To make a leg!

The strangest sight
Since the world began,
The bones all right
To make a man!

v

When all the skeletons
Were done
The busy bones
Grew still again.

As a wood they were
When winter grieves
In the branches bare
Of the shape of leaves.

To give them strength
Then nerve and thew,
Length by length
And two by two,

With a snaky tread
And not a sound
Began to thread
Each bone around!

I hid my face,
I shut my eyes

For the little space
The heart beats thrice,

And then I looked
Again and saw
What is not brooked
By natural law:

Each skull a face,
And trunk and limb
Had the sweet grace
Of flesh on them!

VI

But as I would praise
The miracle
A heavy haze
About me fell.

From the luminous mist
God's voice said:
"They with flesh are dressed,
But they are dead,

"And none can make
Them live but I;
Cease now to quake
And prophesy.

"To the four winds call,
Thou son of man,
That these slain may all
Draw breath again!"

I stood appalled
At His presence hid,
But I called, I called
As I was bid.

From hill and wood
Did the four winds meet,
And the slain all stood
Upon their feet;

An exceeding army,
They drew their breath
And stepped forth free
From the ranks of death!

VII

Ezekiel,
Behold the blood
Of My sons that fall
In the world's dark wood!

Now prophesy
To the troubled host
Whose bones are dry,
Whose hope is lost;

In the battle's shock,
In the ways they grope,
I am their Rock,
I am their Hope!

Their blood I see,
I hear their groans,
Yea, and I am He
That raised the bones!

Of all who went to the woods of Hate
With dog, and gun as well,
Only the meekest will relate
How the foxes ran in hell.

Now, only a morn of the finest frost
Would do for the dogs to run in,
And the time came right and the stars were lost
In a cold and frosty morning.

And the fox rose up from the heavy brush
And the dogs were quick to follow;
And the hunters ran in a cloppy rush
Over ridge and hollow.

The day came up before the sun,
And the hills were hidden under
A sheet of fog, and the sound of a gun
Rang in the air like thunder.

The fox he flashed in the rime-bright air
And the dogs were quick behind him;
And a hunter aimed upon him fair,
But a bullet would not find him.

And the fox he ran, and the dogs they ran,
And the hunters headlong after,
And loud they shouted man to man,
Filling the woods with laughter.

And when the sun was on the rim
Of the hills like a staring eye,

With a fierce black hound by the side of him
A man came running by.

And Orey Duval came suddenly
On the man in the autumn wood,
Leaning against a black gum tree
In a black and terrible mood.

And the man said, "Run as the fox has run
In the blue and bitter air!"
And he snatched forth Duval's horn and gun,
And he leaped on Duval's mare.

And Cedric saw, who was close behind,
That a hound as black as night
Was running as swiftly as the wind
For the devil's own delight.

And a strange man rode on Duval's mare,
Making a loud "Hallo,"
And Cedric heard him whoop and swear
How a fox of hell could go!

And Abner, who came riding next,
Saw Cedric fall to the ground
And rise a fox that was sorely vexed
By a swift and midnight hound.

And Abner had no sooner come
Into the strange man's sight
Than another fox went running home
For the devil's own delight.

And Albert who rode last, and fast
Under the boughs of evil,

23

Swears he rode like a wintry blast
Hunting fox with the devil.

And he came forth from the autumn wood
On a cold and frosty morning
Solitary from solitude,
And he left the foxes running.

And still they say the strange man rides
Hard on his stolen mare,
And the black hound stirs the cold hillsides
With his yelps in the frosty air.

And any man who will go alone
When the day has come to a hush
Can hear the hoofs on the clattering stone,
And the foxes break from the brush!

"Mother, lay the fire again
  And put the kettle on the stove;
  The hills are curtained by the rain,
  And I have lost my love."

"Son, the fire leaps in the grate,
  The kettle whistles through its spout,
  And supper on the board will wait
  Until your story's out."

"Well, Mother, yesterday I saw
  My loved one walking in the hills,
  Twining roses in her hair
  And picking daffodils."

"And there was nothing strange in that.
  Had she no word to say to you
  That you go like an angry cat
  The whole day through?"

"No, Mother, ere the hills became
  Green with the young leaf I was lost
  By looking on a colder flame
  Than burns at the heart of frost.

"And yesterday I saw my love
  With another lover in the wood,
  And who but I should walk with her
  In the green solitude?

"I could not bear to see her bend
  Her lips to another's wooing,

And it was never friend and friend
That kissed as they were doing."

"Stranger things were done, my son;
    Nothing may come of it at last;
So let your head see what is done;
    The heart runs too fast."

"The heart too fast and the feet too fast
    And the hands too fast to slaughter —
Someone seeks in the woods so vast
    Tonight, for a lost daughter.

"And, Mother, lest the lonesome bird
    Haunt me from the willow,
I made her a prayer that no one heard
    And gave her a stone for a pillow.

"Mother, listen to the rain
    That slashes ever harder —
Her handsome lover I have slain
    And left him there to guard her.

"Mother, listen to the night
    That howls about the eaves —
I hid them well and out of sight
    With many little leaves.

"Mother, hush and tend the fire
    And lay the bed with a clean cover;
I sleep tonight with a new desire,
    With a dread and faithful lover."

AMELIA stood
In the quiet grass
Of Coulson's Wood
Where slow winds pass,

And Helmer paced
By her side as though
His hot blood raced
Where the slow winds blow.

Between the two
The grass would bend
As if there blew
A little wind.

Amelia said:
"Though years be fleet
As runners sped
On frightened feet,

"All seeming few
And spoiled and brief,
Each comes anew,
As last year's leaf.

"Our love has made
This moment seem
As aeons stayed
Within a dream."

And Helmer said:
"The grass will die

As days are sped,
And know not why.

"And we no less,
  Though we be brave
  And good, still press
  Unto the grave.

"All things make haste
  As if they yearned
  That rest to taste
  Their toil has earned.

"As birds that sing
  At fall of night,
  When not a-wing,
  Are poised for flight,

"So we confess
  Our feet are shod
  To foot the wilderness
  Of God.

"Though men reprove,
  Pay them no heed:
  Two who will love
  Must love indeed!"

  Between the two
  The grass would bend
  As if unto
  A rising wind.

Amelia said:
"The slow years bless

Two who are wed
With quietness.

"Love's arch of gold
    That girds the heart
    Is strong to hold
    The years apart.

"Love's fruit will hang,
    Though frost be nigh
    And cold clouds billowing
    In the sky,

"Until its taste
    Be made complete,
    Then why make haste
    To pluck and eat?"

And Helmer said:
"The day beats on;
    Morning is quieted
    And gone.

"The sun of noon
    Is hot and high,
    And it will soon
    Desert the sky.

"Evening will paint
    The shore and sea,
    And then grow faint,
    And night will be

"Drawn close about,
    And we shall fear

To wake or shout
Lest death be near.

"The kiss of age
No lip will heed;
Youth's heritage
Is love, indeed!"

Between the two
The grass would bend
As if unto
A wailing wind.

Amelia said:
"Our love must be
Not brought abed
To poverty.

"Although hot blood
Beat at the brain,
Love leaves her hood
Where two have lain.

"Where blind with bliss
To their precipice,
Two lean to kiss
Love leaves her dress.

"Where limbs are sealed
With carnal flame,
Love stands revealed
In naked shame!

"Imperious haste
Pleads not your suit;

Let us not taste
Forbidden fruit."

But Helmer said:
"Take heed of me
Ere I have fled
You utterly:

"My ways are lost,
My footsteps reach,
Beyond the uttermost
Of speech.

"For if one stand
By the water's side
And drown his hand,
Though the banks abide,

"The water goes;
The liquid will
Pulls, and it flows
By plain and hill.

"What things appear
To keep their place
Of far and near
As spaced in space

"Stay not at all,
For hill and town
Spin with this ball
Of earth around;

"And each to each
We look from the eye,

And speak with the speech
Ot a passer-by.

"Thoughts from the mind,
  Love from the heart,
  We wake to find
  That all things part.

"To you, my Love,
  Even now have I
  But time enough
  To say good-bye!"

The sky shone blood,
  And night came on;
  Amelia stood
  In the grass alone.

And ere the dew
  Was dry again,
  A wide wind blew
  Between the twain.

MAY MARGARET

ABOUT the hour the first wind blows
Into the woods of morn
May Margaret stirred herself and rose
And crossed the fields of corn.

The lark was in the lift of day,
His song was clear and keen,
His syllables leant all one way
As windy poplars lean.

Under the little stars of dawn
That button up the sky
She came at length and all alone
Beyond green fields of rye.

Little did she know of what
The deed required for fee
But stepped forth with her evil thought
That stirred incessantly:

The Minister of Trest is tall
And somber in his ways,
And nary a lucky maid at all
Has heard him speak in praise.

Now, could he walk with me at night
And find soft words to say
As do the brawny lads of might
Who talk so hard by day?

Halfway upon the turning road
She halted to return

But listened for the inner goad
And heard it and went on.

Along the river making songs
For what would stop and hear
She fashioned in a thousand tongues
What he would say to her.

And when the sun was nearly gone
She came into the town
And found the Minister alone
In his long black preaching gown.

His eyes were darker than she thought
And his hands were lean and strong,
And she almost lost the aim she brought
So heavily along.

Her hands took refuge in her hair
Blowing so long and loose,
The while she struggled in despair
For a likelier excuse.

"While chopping in the woods today
O'Hara gashed his knee,
And he would have you come and pray
Before his soul must flee."

As they returned by wall and wood
The sky was losing light,
And under the leafy solitude
The air grew dark as night.

Silkily the preacher said,
"My church lies in this wood,

34

And lest O'Hara now be dead
We shall pray for his soul's good."

And once the world was all without
And they alone inside
The preacher said, and turned about,
"This is for what you lied!

"Shortly before you reached my door
All with your lying air,
O'Hara rode to the village store
Sitting his dappled mare!"

His hands went out in search of her,
His lips to hers he bent
And took with trembling and fear
Their lovers' sacrament.

About the hour the last wind blows
Into the day's domain
May Margaret stirred herself and rose
And took the road again.

Among the alders by the road
That skirts the darksome pond
She listened for the inner goad
And heard it and went on.

Her hands took refuge in her hair
Blowing so loose and wild,
And half from guilt and half despair
She sobbed like a frightened child.

Her grief kept whispering on the way,
The thought was grim and hard,

That near-by in the river lay
The fee the deed required.

The water was chilly at the edge
And colder farther in,
And the moon rode there a silver wedge
When the stream grew calm again.

Under the little leaves of life
Helmer rode in a stranger's land,
Bearing beneath his coat a knife
Well fitted to his hand.

The little leaves were green and trim
And the wind was soft and kind,
But shy wild things took flight from him
With murder in his mind.

He left his house, he left his land,
He left his countryside,
With the knife well fitted to his hand,
To seek his wandered bride.

"Her laugh was free, her step was light,
Her eyes outflamed the dawn;
Her lips were wine of a strange delight,"
He mused as he rode on.

"Were she a lesser prize to win,
Or a wench a man would choose
To warm his boughten bed, why then
She were not so much to lose.

"But her love was like a burning bush
On a wide and darkling plain,
Or a voice continually saying *hush*
To whimperings of pain.

"If I have not her warmth by night
Nor her bright look by day

For body's need and soul's delight
I vow no other may.

"I'll search a thousand miles of ground
To be her murderer;
Or if she be by water bound
I'll search the seas for her."

So on he rode both night and day
By alien hill and tree,
Stopping at dwellings by the way
With words of inquiry.

"This lady of the search," said they,
"How shall we know her as
The one you seek; how tell her, pray,
From other maids that pass?"

"Her laugh is free, her step is light,
Her eyes outflame the dawn,
Her lips are wine of a strange delight,"
He said and so rode on.

Beneath the solitudinous boughs
That shake on many a hill
Helmer bore his bitter vows
As an armor to his will.

He sat by many a family fire,
Nor warmth nor bread sought he
But sat thus only to inquire
His ceaseless inquiry.

"This lady, should she come," said they,
"How shall we know her as

The one you seek; how know her, pray,
From any maid that pass?"

"She had a way of making light
  And a way of making dread
  As if a witch or water sprite
  Had lodging in her head."

  And so he rode till autumn flamed
  With crimson shoemake fire;
  And though her name was never named
  He ceased not to inquire.

"This lady of the search," said they,
"How shall we know her as
  The one you seek, if on a day
  She chance this way to pass?"

"To cold she is the warming sun,
  To desert thirst, a flood;
  She is the cool of summer dawn,
  And a fever in the blood."

  Among the little rounded hills
  That step up from the sea
  He rested on the brown pine spills
  To make his inquiry.

"A twelvemonth past she came," they said,
"But she has journeyed on,
  Singing upon a road that led
  Into the gates of dawn."

"A six-month past she came," they said,
"But vanished with the spring,

Sighing upon a road that led
To the halls of evening."

"A fortnight gone she came," they said,
"Your lady of delight,
Crying most dismally, and sped
Into the windy night."

And when he questioned by the way
Where highland poplars wave:
"News of her death had we," said they,
"But no one knows her grave."

Then Helmer rode most bitterly
Into a winter dawn;
"I've sought her through the earth," said he,
"I'll seek her now beyond."

But whether wind blow north or west
Or whether east or south,
The knife he bore is in his breast,
The mould is on his mouth;

And what pale palfrey shall he ride,
What magic-metalled knife
Have power to harm his wandered bride
Beyond the leaves of life!

BALLAD OF THE WEAVER

OLD Margot, the weaver,
Grows slow at the loom
As the thread flies over
The shuttle of doom.

Her fingers have guided
The pearly wool thread
That shroud has provided
The long-sleeping dead.

Her quick foot has treadled,
Her brown fingers styled
The warm cloth that swaddled
The new-crying child.

She has spun in the harness
Cloth, lovely and wide,
White gowning to bless
The first night of the bride.

And jeans she has woven,
For many a groom,
Whose thread is spun thin on
The shuttle of doom.

To curtain the vision
Of love, new and kind,
The cloth of derision
She wove in her mind.

And yet as she fingers
The bright, flowing thread,

Her spinning thought lingers
With the lost or the dead,

With pains to discover
The rapture she knew
When night did not cover
One sleeper, but two.

Her cat hardly stirs
To be hearing again
The fall of her tears
Like a thin summer rain.

He knows from much telling
How when she was young
One came to her dwelling
With a smile and a song.

She loved him for graces
The traveler knows,
And for dust of far places
That clung to his clothes.

And all to discover
What many have known:
Whose lord is a rover
Her house keeps alone.

He rode from her humming
A tune full of tears;
And she waited his coming
And counted the years

That she had waited,
And he not come,

Till five had freighted
Each finger and thumb.

She speaks through the whirring
Of shuttle and thread,
And the cat, on hearing,
Has lifted his head:

"The thread is thinning;
My shroud is spun;
The weaving and spinning
Are over and done!"

The thread of her will
Has snapped in the loom;
Her foot has grown still
On the treadle of doom.

AMELIA said,
Half under her breath,
"Now Barker is dead,
And I have no bread."
Hunger and grief
Are dowers of death.

"Since Barker lies lonely
Six by three
Life is only
Pain to me,"
Amelia said
Upon her knee.

Summer and winter
Blew mild and wild.
Amelia's grief
Renewed with the leaf
But to outward view
She was reconciled.

Carlton came
To mend and to plow,
And say with her name,
"It is over now;
Grief is a flame
That time brings low."

Amelia weighed
Her heart's distress
Against her need,
And found it less

A thing to heed
Than happiness.

Amelia said
As Carlton's bride:
"I shall be fed
And loved beside —
Grief is a scar
The heart can hide."

I

O Laurie, I hear
A cry on the air,
And it is half fear
And half despair.

Laurie, go look
To see if a child
Is lost by the brook
That waters the wild.

And I will go see
If anything lost
Is sunk to the knee
In water and frost.

II

O Laurie, I saw
A beast by a tree
That held in its maw
A figure like me;

And I was crying
From misery and fear
In syllables dying,
And none to hear.

And, Laurie, you wept
From a similar place,
So lonely I kept
My eyes from your face.

And, Laurie, you bled,
But I could not move;
And then you were dead —
O horror of love!

III

"I found by a stream
A road from this wood;
In waters of dream
I saw how we stood

Secure from the cry
Of misery and fear.
A bird went by
On the tides of the air

Crying in syllables
Of sound
So sweet I fell
Upon the ground

To hear him sing,
But on he went
On subtle wing
As if intent

On guiding me.
I followed and heard
The prophecy
Of Love's proud bird

In woods no dismal
Night can claim.
I heard him call
And knew his name.

Can you not guess
This was the dove,
Symbol to bless
Our feast of love?"

IV

O Laurie, I fear
Your dream was a myth,
A song in your ear
From the daughter of death.

For clearly I saw
Destruction and woe
Await in the maw
Of the beastly foe;

And doom a ghastly
Curtain to drape
Us who would lastly
Seek escape.

How shall we cause
The water to know
That breakers of laws
Are marked for woe;

Or how declare
The hesitant word
To tides of the air
That carried the bird?

How shall we explain
The messenger ill
That speaks from the brain
Of two on a hill;

Oh, and how shall we make
A respectable dove
To sing for the sake
Of a shameless love?

v

"If I am to die
In the dark of the night
Why should I not lie
In the arms of delight?

If you are to wail
My loss to the wind
Why should you not hail
Me other than friend;

Why should you not cry
My name to the town
From the hill that is high
Over two going down?

The law that I claim,
For happiness' sake,
Is to serve in the name
Of what I can take;

And you I shall have
If might can make right.
Wild demons that rave
Me news in the night

Declare I may take
Of you, O Clod,
And die for the sake
Of a lesser than God!"

49

O Laurie, I swear
My will is most broke;
I long for your hair
Soft under my stroke.

I ache for your limbs
Soft over my side;
And darkness that dims
For the sake of a bride.

I long for and sigh,
I ache for your breath
Between my lips — I
Have no business with death!

VII

Over this way
Go largest and least;
And Bird and the day,
And night and the Beast.

As lonely listeners
We may sigh
Or quake to hear
The Beast cry.

But from a distance
We have heard
— If only once —
The singing Bird!

A SONG OF SORROW

O MEN, come in from the field and the lane
And pray over Sarah's one daughter again
For she is possessed of a terrible pain.

O men, come in and softly abide
In reverent silence with your knees spread wide
For Sarah's one daughter has suffered and died.

O men, come in from the field and the plow
And pick at your teeth with the tip of a bough,
And say to her kindly brave words for tomorrow
For Sarah's possessed of a pitiful sorrow.

ALL THE LEAVES IN THE WILDWOOD

WHEN softly from the shuttered east
The eye of day began to stare
We crossed the fields, and saw the beasts
All lying close together there.
And farther on where trembling lay
The shadows at the feet of day
The fallen vines, the green leaves wist
How she and I with our lips kissed
And lightly went upon our way.

We made no sound at all upon
The green leaves of the forest floor,
And as we walked the brooks that run
Forbade her wade them, so I bore
Her in my arms; and in the mist
The thin green leaves of the wildwood wist
How she and I with our lips kissed
And went on lightly to our door.

We made a cup of the wildwood leaves
And filled it with the water clear,
And where the stone the water cleaves
She drank and I drank after her.
The hushed air made no slightest stir,
And lightly in the morning mist
All the leaves in the wildwood wist
How she and I with our lips kissed
And parted with no more than that.

THEY go together,
As lovers should,
And take of their love
In the shade of the wood.

It is not ugly,
Nor is it unclean
To lie in the shadow
Unknown and unseen.

Never a sorrow
Was born of two
Couched in the shadow
The whole night through.

If only lovers
Walked in the lane
No one would suffer
Or sorrow again;

But a step before them
And a step behind
Are people possessed
Of a very small mind

Who nod and whisper,
And poison the bread
Of innocent lovers
Until they are dead.

IN HIDING

As I came riding
By Malvern Hill
One came from hiding
In the woods so still.

I drew rein to tease him
And mutter him a rhyme,
And promise I would please him
In God's good time.

But bitter is the biding,
Bitter and in vain:
He is in hiding
By every path and lane.

BITTER BERRY

The voice of the water
Crying on a stone
Said to Helmer's daughter
Sitting alone:

"Death itself is mellow
When age has ripened one,
But death's a bitter berry
In the morning of the sun."

And so to Helmer's daughter,
The youngest one of all,
The green untimely berry
Was as bitter as gall.

I took my fiddle
That sings and cries
To a hill in the middle
Of Paradise.

I sat at the base
Of a golden stone
In that holy place
To play alone.

I tuned the strings
And began to play,
And a crowd of wings
Were bent my way.

A voice said
Amid the stir:
"We that were dead,
 O Fiddler,

"With purest gold
 Are robed and shod,
 And we behold
 The face of God.

"Our halls can show
 No thing so rude
 As your horsehair bow,
 Or your fiddlewood;

"And yet can they
 So well entrance
 If you but play
 Then we must dance!"

II

FROM SLEEP THE MADRIGALS

Far off high misty madrigals
Wake in the cloudy atmosphere
Of leaf-light under rain that falls
    Gently O
Through the darkening air.
Gathered to little rivers down
Each gully, forth the water bears
Whatever it dislodge or drown,
Blossom or ant, or my own prayers
Fallen beyond me like a leaf
Surrendered to the will of wind.
An air itinerant and brief
Scarfs the slow dripping from the hedge;
And when the day is at an end
I hear from sleep's remotest edge
The singer, busy with his say
From which I shall not rest again:
A journey across an endless plain,
A traveler on a lonesome way.

INVOCATION

O Song, hung as clear in the mind
As the tremor of beaten bells,
Come forth now, lovely and clear,
And undisturbed by the swells
Of the ocean of thought that beats
On the shores of a troubled year.
Let what the tongue repeats
Of evil and death be drowned
By a lovelier sound.

I AM THE DUST

I AM the dust made animate,
Earth's singer given syllables,
As Homer of an elder date,
For sorrow, joy and love and hate
And greetings and farewells.

Too soon I too shall be as quiet
As they who know not how the night
Is dark nor how the day is clear,
But for a fleeting moment yet
I traffic with the alphabet
Before I am anonymous
And scattered everywhere.

SEND FORTH THE HUNTER

SEND forth the hunter into the wilderness,
    Send him forth into the mind's prairie,
To seek the quarry that shall not grow less
    Though he grow lean and weary.

The hunted slip soft-shod into the night
    Not more nor less for having disappeared,
Nor less delightful that the hunter's sight
    Has lost them, as he feared.

Send forth the hunter into the thicketed mind.
    Dim and uncertain are the ways that front
Hunter and quarry that he may not find,
    But send him forth to hunt.

WISDOM

THOUGH aimless as the sun or wind
Observe how agile is the mind.
A silver fish with silver fin
The roving mind moves out and in
Among the roots of things to learn.
A swimmer in an earthen urn
The mind goes slyly on its way,
But by what paths it does not say;
And sounds that it will never tell
Trouble the water, like a bell
Warning the mind that it should shun
A shore already touched upon.

IN THE MIND'S MEADOW

HERE in the mind's meadow no day shall turn
The thought stems dry, no fire shall burn
Through dust-dry stubble;
But there shall be water in plenty
For the growing thought till one is twenty.

I have heard it said that no rain falls
In the mind's meadow, that no bird calls
From the flowering spray after one is twenty.
These words are spoken, but not by the old;
Their dry minds know their damp days
Though the rain is cold.

HOUSE IN THE WIND

SINCE life is a house in the wind
Leaning against the cold
In which the body hides,
I wonder if he is bold

Who opens the subtle door
And looks upon the sky
Beyond his narrow house,
Even though he must die.

For ever this remains
A thing to think about:
Whether a man is better in
His house, or better out.

SPACIAL INTERLUDE

HELMER looked upon the day
From a wall outside the sun,
Facing east for half the way
Where the west is but begun.

Helmer watched oncoming night
Flowing like a sea of mud
Over eastern islands bright
Till he saw the growing flood

Rushed from the enormous mouth
Of the caverned evening sky
Fall to east of west, and south
Of the north, and so go by.

THE FRUIT AND THE BOUGH

TIME hangs, a ripe fruit in the wind,
As if it would soon be down;
But the world runs on to its end,
And man, no less for his dreams
And books and laws, to the ground.

And when God comes to shake
The boughs where hangs his fruit,
Little and big and all,
It will be last to break,
Under his impetuous foot
It will be last to fall.

WE SHALL NOT EAT

WE shall not eat of the fruit
Hanging delicious and high,
We shall look up and dispute
Which is the sky.

We shall not eat of the meat
Graceful and shy on the hoof,
It shall be roving and fleet
And we aloof.

We shall not eat of the bread
But the want of it will sing,
And lonely and shy and unfed
We shall go forth hungering.

In orchards hung with fruit,
With purple globes and gold,
From mountains to the sea,
The blight, the brute,
Now as of old
Will be.

And next spring, as of old,
The enemy will devour
The fruit within the flower
— Save what escapes to mould
And sour.

THE HARVEST: 1942

Spring was the perilous season,
And sowers that entered the gate
Were plowing the earth with treason
And scattering seeds of hate.

And now the harvest is ready,
And I with foreclosured breath
Must rise from my dreams unsteady
And reap with a sickle of death.

HAVING been concerned with trees
That lean but break not with the storm;
And having known, other than trees,
Those like myself in form,
The old and the sorely tried,
The yet unbroken despite
That years they have long defied
Have snowed them white;

Shall the mind in its twenty-fifth year
Under its raven hair
Begin so soon to despair,
Surrender so soon to fear
In this blind and bloody year?

III

THE DAWN CAME DOWN

THE round day was a circus tent
Across whose top the sun
Crawled like a fly on fiery legs.
But when the day was done
The night stretched out unendingly,
And I could scarce recall
Whether or not upon this spot
The dawn came down at all.

APPLE PICKING

AUTUMN frosts the hedges,
The cricket plays his flute,
And high on ladder-ledges
The pickers pluck the fruit.

Before the sun has faded
Beyond the edge of day
The orchard is denuded,
The apples stored away;

Except those left to wither
And feed the sluggish bee
Because no hand could gather
Them from the tallest tree!

SUMMER

This is the season
Most men declare,
For a weighty reason,
To be most fair.

The food for winter
On branch and vine
For picker and vintner
The days entwine.

The golden apple
And waving corn
The bright dews dapple
At early morn.

Even the mice
Make glee that here
Is food for thrice
Their needs this year.

And cautious crows
Alight and steal
Among the rows
Of the farmer's field.

But a windy rumor
Through field and town
Says the leaves of summer
Have been thrown down.

WHOSE EYE IS ON THE
SPARROW

I SAW a fallen sparrow
Dead upon the grass
And mused to see how narrow
The wing that bore it was.

By what unlucky chance
The bird had come to settle
Lopsided near the fence
In sword grass and nettle

I had no means to know;
But this I minded well:
Whose eye was on the sparrow
Shifted, and it fell.

ANALOGY AT A DESERTED HOUSE

BEAUTIFUL at nightfall about the empty house
The rose and the wind conspire to fill the air,
And meekly from his hole a soft, timid mouse
Slips through the dusk to find his supper there.

One lone hollyhock bends to the green
Grass that is tumbled and long and unshorn,
But not a face at the window is seen
At darkness or morn.

The last word said there fell in the grass,
Only a whisper that no one has heard,
And even the speaker forgot what it was
When the grass was stirred.

AUTUMN MOOD

THE leaf flies from the stricken bough,
The aster blows alone;
And in the curve of heaven now
The wild geese tread the dawn.

I would I had no ears to hear
And had no eyes to see
What is so beautiful and dear
Escaping me!

YEAR'S ENDING

WIND must enter
    The heart now
For the breath of winter
    Is cold to the brow.

And the voice of winter
    Is loud in the garden
Where dead flowers enter
    The earth and harden.

The snow that is shaken
    From silver trees
Must surely waken
    The soul from ease;

For the voice of winter
    Is loud in the heart
Where no love blooms
    And no dreams start.

73

SEASONAL

ALTHOUGH it is not in the mind
For youth to be brief as the summer
Earth's seasons are all of a kind.
     The earliest comer
To spring must witness the bough
Translate the blooming that dapples
The land untouched by the plow,
To the falling of apples.

I GO BY WAYS OF RUST AND FLAME

I GO by ways of rust and flame
Beneath the bent and lonely sky;
Behind me on the ways I came
I see the hedges lying bare,
But neither question nor reply.

A solitary thing am I
Upon the roads of rust and flame
That thin at sunset to the air.
I call upon no word nor name,
And neither question nor reply
But walk alone as all men must
Upon the roads of flame and rust.

SONG AFTER HARVEST

Now we are done with the last bundle
Of rye and wheat.
What was green in the fields of spring
And bronze in summer's
Is now meal in the barrel
Or bread to eat.

This was no labor of love
But sweat will sweeten
The bread from the salted brow;
When the snows come
We will give grave thanks for the bread, eaten
To the last crumb.

God of the hunted,
Of the harried creatures,
Deflect the bullet.

God of the leaf
The deer comes under
In the hurried thunder
Of his bright hoof,
Destroy the scent;
Let the dog's deep bay
Be far away.
Let the spotted fawn
Lie alone
Under the boughs bent.

God of the grain
Where quail lie hidden,
Keep their small plain
To men forbidden.
Let hunters chase
A phantom's features
And leave in peace
The harried creatures.
Deflect the bullet,
God of the hunted!

BOY AND DEER

OVER the white, the frozen ground
With cautious step the deer came down.

The boy who had come to be
Alone with cloud and rock and tree

Suddenly saw the deer and hid
To see what that proud creature did.

But the sharp snapping of a limb
Made the proud deer aware of him.

Kindred two, each watcher stood
With perfect stillness in the wood,

Each seeing each with mild surprise,
And each with wonder in his eyes.

A BOY SINGS TO THE WIND

THE wind sings on the hill
   Where a lad dreams in the sun
   And he and the sky are one
And he and the sky are still.

And the wind sings to the lad
   From lorn lands of the sun
   And he and the wind are one
And he and the wind are sad.

This they do in the end,
   Lock hands and sing together,
   But in the calmer weather
The boy sings to the wind.

A YOUTH SPEAKS TO AN ELDER

Now, if you were Richard or if you were Will,
Or if you were a lone voice lost on a hill
I would hear you and give you my aid
Unreservedly, and quite unafraid.

But you are not Richard, nor either of these,
But an old, old man with rheumatic knees,
And I shall not aid you, and I shall not be kind,
Lest you should stab me with a knife from behind.

IV

A BOY'S WEATHER

I KNOW how it seems within a boy's head,
Having myself been young not long ago,
Nothing is finer, after all is said,
Weather has power to offer than a snow.
A shower may prove a respite from the field
But only briefly, and it clogs his feet
When he returns, it is a drudge concealed;
Only a snow is perfect and complete.

No sooner is November's lease secure
And the first snowflakes are a prophecy,
Than he must rise at night and see for sure
Whether they mean to speak the truth or lie;
Seeing white proof the flakes meant what they said
He shuts the shutters and goes back to bed.

If man might lean his elbows on the sky
As farmers lean their weight upon a wall
To look upon their ample fields that lie
Heavy with harvest in the yellow Fall,
Then he might dicker with close-fisted fate,
Himself decide what to reject or keep
Before he comes at length beyond the gate
Where he may choose not anything but sleep.

Yet if he leaned but once upon a star
And saw his earth, and himself fugitive,
As long as breath could keep life's door ajar
He would be happy but to breathe and live,
With little care for what he shall be when
Of death's gray waste he is a citizen.

HAVING unloosed the foxes of the mind
To run about the margins of the world,
With the five hounds the sense has close behind,
The hunter who in his eagerness has hurled
Himself astride the swift, unsaddled wind,
Fit charger for so furious a chase,
Shall be companioned by no easy friend;
To alien vistas he shall turn his face.

Yet he shall feel a surging in his blood
Like troubled water at the flush of spring,
And know it clean and vigorous and good;
And as his mount streaks through the evening
He shall behold upon a darkening hill
The hounds yet fleet, the foxes fleeter still.

MY LOVE IS FAIRER

My love is fairer than a plum in bloom
Amid dun thickets of the upland sorrel;
Fairer she is than bluets in the broom,
Fairer than waxen trumpets of the laurel.
Fairer my love is than the burdened rose,
Fairer than bluebells in the lily's shadow;
Fairer indeed than anything that grows
After the spring has wakened field and meadow.

Yet love itself is very like a flower,
Even as the kept word of the poets teach,
A thing of beauty in a barren land —
But not to be possessed before that hour
When the rash seeker, in his avid reach,
Against its stem of life has scored his hand.

BURIAL OF EARTH

AFTER the beech was all that held its leaves
Against the wind, against the coming on
Of lessening days when every dusk retrieves
A colder sharpness than day had at dawn,
Suddenly the brooks were under ice,
And their low mumbling proclaimed them lost
Beneath the white and twofold artifice
Forged in the chilly foundry of the frost.
Yet the earth lived beneath its ragged cape
Of leaf and mould until the circled moon
Surrendered up its poor pale borrowed heat
And fled, with its star ally, to escape
The cloud that bore the first snowfall, and soon
Burial of earth and water was complete.

LIFE IS THE LODGER

THE wind today blows bitterly north by west
Against the shaken walls of a lonely dwelling
Whose lodger within is a timid if stalwart guest
Who lives in a room, but which there is no way of telling.
A bitter wind, a wind with a lonesome cry
Strives at the two high windows that look from the tower
Until the night to live, and the day to die,
Come to the selfsame spot at the selfsame hour.

A curious house is this which the wind assaults
As if it were only a fort besieged by winter,
Planned with infinite care from roof to floor
And perfectly, too, except for these two faults:
The tenant at will can neither leave it nor enter,
And once without he can never reopen the door!

MEDITATION

ALL things grow old, reach their appointed end,
Wear out, grow useless or at best inept,
Even as a man forgets his boyhood friend
And a child, grown up, lays by the toys he kept.
Dust in the kingdoms where great kings have slept
Defines them lastly; and their works are hurled
To rust and ruin where fierce winds have swept
The outward edges of the turning world.

Time has stored many in a little room.
Helen and all of Troy are nothing now
But words grown feeble and a little dull
From much repeating. But the face of Doom,
Now that we see it, has a noble brow
And, even to youth, eyes not unbeautiful.

MONOCHORD

TROUBLE, I heard the wind say to the tree,
Trouble and death and a red tide of blood;
Trouble, O trouble by the surging sea,
Trouble and anguish in the silent wood.
Trouble, the wind said, blood upon the wheat;
Sorrow, it said, death in the narrow sky;
Horror, it said, given as bread to eat
Unto the young that they may ail and die.

Tidings of terror like a brazen horn,
Blood on the waters where the hosts are slain;
Trouble, the wind said moving in the corn,
Trouble, O trouble on the heaving plain;
Trouble and death the day that man was born
— How shall the earth be free of him again!

THE HEART AS A BIRD

O Heart, be swift, a bird to rise and soar;
Death follows after thee from every bough.
I read from runes of earth how once Death swore
Unto the end of time a fatal vow:
"Not one of all earth's creatures, foul or fair,
Neither the plain nor comely shall escape;
Though even the leper shun me in his lair,
Though I be held a pale unfinite shape,
A sleep, a dream, for who admits me other?
A lying down, a dusky interval
I made a covenant with Life, my brother,
Into my hands he will betray them all!"
Therefore, poor Heart, be swift to wing another
And yet another league before you fall.

BEFORE the bullet yet has left the muzzle
But makes its perilous stay within the barrel
A fleeting pause before its point will nuzzle
The yielding flesh with which it has no quarrel,
The laboring heart is busy in its tower
Sending its envoy forth to every cell.
Fleet diplomat sent from the sovereign power
To its satellites with a fearful thing to tell,
The blood proclaims before it hurries on:
The enemy is pressing hard at hand,
You are outweaponed, your defense is gone,
Defeat is certain, yet you are to stand . . .
And then it halts in what it meant to say
As death arrives that was but on the way.

ADDRESS TO THE HEART

INDUSTRIOUS heart, from your hid anchorage
In the ribbed side, beat out the conscious day;
And when night shuts from view the well-read page,
Sleep clothes the mind in thoughtless ecstasy
And limbs can lie unhurried and relaxed —
However weary of your stroke you be,
Or weak or ailing, tired or overtaxed,
Beat on, beat on in your dim cavity.

The eyes, being tired, may draw their shutters to,
Tired feet find comfort in the stride's decrease,
The mind in sleep seeks out a place apart
For its renewal — all these rest, but you
Have not that privilege until you cease,
Therefore be resolute, industrious heart!

SONNET MODELED ON

AN AILING HEART

WHAT shall be said to the heart that bides its time
To abdicate its throne, resign its power?
Wait till the hand has written out its rhyme;
Wait till the spring is finished with the flower.
Say to it: Wait, there is no need to hasten!
Say: There is time enough when the hair is white
To abdicate, resign, depart, and fasten
The final door against all sound and light.

What shall be said to the heart that has given warning
It means to cease, has warned of intended treason?
Beg it ask not of the sun that it set in the morning,
Beg it be faithful yet for a day, a season;
Pray it shut not the mouth on the taste of hunger;
Pray it beat longer, longer, a little longer!

BY THE WATERS OF LIFE

My servant, blood, be chary of all haste;
Flow not a whit the faster for hate or love,
The one would stain a knife point with your waste,
The other too swift a pace would have you move.
For all love prates of how her heart is kind,
For all hate thinks itself a fearful force,
To one unfeeling, to the other, blind,
Flow without hindrance on your charted course.

My sanguine friend, be placid in your path,
Flow as a brook that is not slow nor fleet
But of one measure all the summer day;
For since each heartbeat drives you nearer death,
That solemn destination, is it meet
Either to speed or loiter on the way!